IMAGES
of America

SOUTH SHORE

RHODE ISLAND

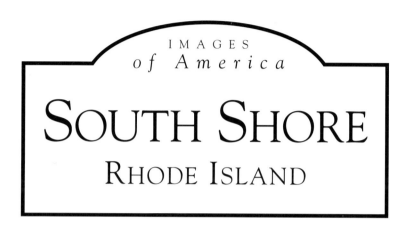

IMAGES
of America

SOUTH SHORE
RHODE ISLAND

Betty J. Cotter

ARCADIA

Copyright © 1999 by Betty J. Cotter.
ISBN 0-7524-1295-7

Published by Arcadia Publishing,
an imprint of Tempus Publishing, Inc.
2 Cumberland Street
Charleston, SC 29401

Printed in Great Britain.

Library of Congress Catalog Card Number: 99-62772

For all general information contact Arcadia Publishing at:
Telephone 843-853-2070
Fax 843-853-0044
E-Mail edit@arcadiaimages.com

For customer service and orders:
Toll-Free 1-888-313-BOOK

Visit us on the internet at http://www.arcadiaimages.com

CONTENTS

ACKNOWLEDGMENTS

This work would not have been possible without the generosity of the area's photograph and postcard collectors, libraries, and historical societies. Many whose materials I borrowed were those whom I had met at book signings for earlier books in this series. They all are lovers of history, and I am grateful for their willingness to help me.

First and foremost I wish to thank Elaine Pereira, who let me borrow more than 70 images from her postcard collection and whose contributions form a large part of this book. I am also deeply indebted to the following people, some of whom also provided caption information: the Charlestown Historical Society and its president, Geneva DeWolf; Linda Stedman; Christine MacManus; my aunt, Dorothy Crandall Bliss; Dot Smith; Judith A. Babcock; Everett Hopkins; Laura Harris of FourQuest Entertainment; John W. Miller Jr.; Charlotte Brophy; Lee Gilson Dursin; Marie Casey; Mercedes McCabe; Dianne McHugh and the Robert Beverly Hale Library; Joan W. Nippo; Daniel G. Dunn; Daryl Anderson; J.A. Coggeshall; and Barbara and Wallace Burdick.

For proofreading assistance, I wish to thank Diane Smith and Barbara and Wallace Burdick.

For information on the cover photograph, see pp. 22–23.

INTRODUCTION

The story of South County's shore resorts is one of discovery, decline, change, and rediscovery. As early as the pre-Civil War period visitors began to discover the attractions Rhode Island's Atlantic Coast afforded in the balmy summer months. At first they came in wagons and stagecoaches to stay in modest farmhouses that had been converted to boardinghouses for the season. Gradually, entrepreneurs began to discover that the bigger and better the accommodations, the more visitors they could attract; soon they began to make actually getting to South County easier, too, with trolley lines, steamer docks, and railroad spurs off the main corridor. Competition among resorts was keen, and each had its own characteristics, appealing to different visitors depending on their income and desires. Did they want a quiet place of rest or a social whirl? Where were they on the social ladder?

South County resorts never quite rivaled Newport, although perhaps some Watch Hill residents would dispute this—or declare themselves grateful for it. Narragansett Pier perhaps came close. In his rating of Eastern resorts in 1908, Frank Crowinshield included the Pier, with this comment: "Geographically speaking, this is nearly Newport, but the social tone, though 'nobby,' can hardly be called A-1." Other resorts were completely off the social map for some, although prized by others for their very remoteness.

Besides social requirements, visitors were concerned about their health. Indeed, the healthful aspects of Rhode Island's resorts were almost always cited in promotional literature. Perhaps it is understandable that as Eastern cities became more industrialized and, thus, polluted, the elite would look forward to escaping to the cleaner air and waters of shoreline towns. Hotels often mentioned the purity of their water in advertisements, claiming it came from this or that spring, and the curative aspects of the salt air were much touted. "Sanitary arrangements" and "pure water" were listed alongside spacious accommodations and delicious food as important attributes of the big hotels.

Summer cottages came next, although the name would seem a misnomer for many of these estates. Houses on the beachfront were the next step for those tired of spending an entire season in a hotel and whose growing wealth needed an outlet. But the biggest change to the area's resorts would come from the automobile, which made Americans more mobile and less inclined to stay for one season in one place, and brought the shore within reach of more, and less socially connected, people. Thus tourist camps, courts, clam shacks, luncheonettes, and general stores, which served their patrons, began to crop up all along the shore. No longer was enjoyment of a summer by the sea the sovereign of the wealthy.

A decline in wealth, particularly after the stock market crash of 1929, would hurt resorts already struggling with changing demographics. The Hurricane of 1938 would wipe the slate clean for the resorts that still hung on, dealing a bitter and tragic blow to an area already past its glory years.

Vestiges of this grand past remain from Watch Hill Point to Narragansett Pier, and today tourists—and new residents—have rediscovered the charms of living by the sea and salt ponds. May we all never forget the many evolutions of our South Shore.

Betty J. Cotter
February 1999

One

ALONG THE
OLD POST ROAD

The Village Street, Charlestown, R. I.

In many ways the history of the South Shore has been written along the Old Post Road. Laid out about 1703 and cut into pieces during the construction of Route 1 in the 1960s, the road that Ben Franklin traveled in the 18th century still brings visitors to South County on its meandering route from Westerly to Wakefield. This view of the road was taken in Cross' Mills; the village's Baptist church can be seen in the distance. (Courtesy Elaine Pereira.)

This is a closer view of the Cross' Mills Baptist Church and the Cross' Mills Public Library. The First Baptist Church and Society at Cross' Mills built this sanctuary in 1873 at a cost of about $1,500 after acquiring the land from George Burdick. The Charlestown Library Association was established in 1849–50 but the tiny library was not built until 1913. William Franklin Tucker, in his *Historical Sketch of the Town of Charlestown*, wrote that the library had been established with "500 good books" and as of his writing, in 1877, boasted 650 volumes. (Courtesy Charlestown Historical Society.)

Coronation Rock, at King Tom Farm on Old Post Road in Charlestown, was the site of the Narragansett Indians' royal coronations. Here Queen Esther was crowned in 1770 to succeed her brother, King Thomas Ninigret. (Courtesy Charlestown Historical Society.)

OLD WILCOX TAVERN – Charlestown, Rhode Island – at the Monument on U. S. Scenic Route 1

The Wilcox Tavern, built probably in the 1730s, has been known variously as the Monument House—for the monument to Joseph Stanton next to it—and the Joseph Stanton House. Its public use dates to its purchase in 1811 by Edward Wilcox, and by 1820 it was an important stagecoach stop. Another phase in its public life began in the 1930s when Dr. Fritz Swanson opened it as the Old Wilcox Tavern, a use it retains to this day. (Courtesy Elaine Pereira.)

This 18th-century inn, the General Stanton Inn on Old Post Road in Charlestown, is the namesake of Gen. Joseph Stanton, although he was not its first owner, having acquired the house in the 1790s. With a varied history as a political gathering place and reputed gambling joint (in the 1920s), the General Stanton Inn today is an inn and restaurant and its property is the site of a popular weekend flea market. (Courtesy Barbara and Wallace Burdick.).

11

King Tom Farm was built between 1746 and 1769 by Thomas "King Tom" Ninigret, a Narragansett Indian who had brought his home plans to Charlestown after a stay in England. The property was sold to settle family debts in 1773. (Courtesy Charlestown Historical Society.)

This is what King Tom Farm looked like after the original house burned in 1922 and was replaced with a neo-Colonial house a year later. The house was in the Kenyon family until 1939. (Courtesy Charlestown Historical Society.)

This group is gathered in front of the original Perryville Baptist Church on Old Post Road in Perryville, sometime before the building was replaced in 1906. The people in the photograph are, from left to right, Leroy Carpenter, the Reverend Peckham, J. Whitford, N.M. Carpenter, M. Gould, ? Gould, M. Browning, ? Boucher, unidentified, ? Tucker, Edith ?, two unidentified, George W. Whitford, W.E. Whitford, Howard Browning, George Kelly, and ? Clarke. (Courtesy Everett Hopkins.)

The Perryville Baptist Church, today a private residence, has long been an imposing structure on Old Post Road in Perryville. The structure preceding this one was built in 1845, two years after the congregation formed. When Henry Jackson visited the sanctuary for his 1853 survey of Baptist churches in the state, he noted, "This church promises well and needs encouragement. They have a property, as per tax list, of $34,000 only." At the time of his visit the congregation numbered 150. It was replaced by the church pictured here in 1906, according to historian Oliver Stedman. (Courtesy Elaine Pereira.)

The Perryville Baptist Church can be seen in this bucolic picture of Perryville. According to historian Oliver Stedman, the village originally was called "Perrysville." Old Post Road still looks much as it does in this postcard. (Courtesy Joan W. Nippo.)

Charles B. Champlin, pictured here, lived in the red cottage on Old Post Road, which gave the intersecting Red House Road its name. Champlin's son, George I. Champlin, founded Dewey Cottage in Matunuck in 1898. (Courtesy Joan W. Nippo.)

Summer Residence of Rev. Dr. Edward Everett Hale, Showing Pond. Matunuck, R. I.

Edward Everett Hale, author, Unitarian minister, and chronicler of his time, found respite in the Matunuck Hills off Old Post Road in this house built as a gift from his friend and neighbor, William B. Weeden. Beginning in 1873, the Hales and their seven children came to Matunuck each summer to pick berries, row on Wash Pond (which they nicknamed Sybaris Lake, after Hale's version of utopia), paint, and write. Their beloved "lake" can be seen here in the foreground. (Courtesy Elaine Pereira.)

Summer Residence of Rev. Dr. Edward Everett Hale. Matunuck, R. I.

This photograph shows another view of the Hale home. The tragic death of the Hales' son, Robert Beverly Hale, in 1895 just as his writing career had begun led to the establishment of the nearby Robert Beverly Hale Library. The library was built on land donated by William B. Weeden and Charles Matlack and was dedicated in 1897. (Courtesy Everett Hopkins.)

15

Summer Residence of Wm. B. Weeden. Matunuck, R. I.

William B. Weeden, friend and business partner to Edward Everett Hale, acquired this house in 1853. It had been in the Weeden family since 1826 and a family member had nicknamed it "Willow Dell." (Courtesy Elaine Pereira.)

12344—Birthplace of Commodore Perry, Metunic, R. I.

Long believed to be the birthplace of naval war hero Oliver Hazard Perry, this gambrel-roofed cottage off Old Post Road had become a tourist attraction by the time the Works Progress Administration's Federal Writers' Project was writing its guide to Rhode Island. The guide, written in 1937, notes that the house was open to the public from May 30 to October 1, with admission ranging from 25¢ to 50¢. There is no historical evidence that Perry was born in the house; indeed, some believe he was born in the Rocky Brook section of Peace Dale. (Courtesy Elaine Pereira.)

16

In later years Matunuck Hills became a popular summer colony, prized for the breathtaking views of Matunuck and the Atlantic Ocean to the south and for the privacy it afforded. This cottage was owned by the Goodchild family. (Courtesy Mercedes McCabe.)

This photograph gives another view of the Goodchild estate. (Courtesy Robert Beverly Hale Library.)

The Homestead in Matunuck is bustling with activity in this photograph, probably shortly after the turn of the century. This house, later the Breezy Acres Tourist Home, was torn down to make way for the construction of Route 1, according to Russell W. Brown. (Courtesy Elaine Pereira.)

This is the Homestead after it became Breezy Acres Tourist Home, located on Old Post Road in Matunuck. The postcard describes the establishment as "a clean, comfortable home in the country, equipped with modern bathrooms and Beautyrest mattresses." (Courtesy Elaine Pereira.)

Two

BATHING BEAUTIES

The True sisters of Hope Valley take a dip in the Atlantic Ocean, their dresses gathered practically for the occasion. The ocean has inspired man and woman alike to don all manner of costumes with which to enjoy its waters. (Courtesy Christine MacManus.)

WATCH HILL, R. I.   BATHING BEACH AND LARKIN HOUSE.

Bathers stroll the beach in front of Larkin House at Watch Hill. The big hotels, which became popular in the late 19th century, placed vacationers squarely on the oceanfront for the first time. Larkin House was the largest hotel in Watch Hill when J.R. Cole was writing his history of Washington and Kent counties in 1889. Built in 1868, the hotel by 1889 had been added to four times and could house 400 guests. Cole described its rooms as "large, with high ceilings, airy and well furnished." (Courtesy Elaine Pereira.)

Matunuck's beachfront was much more ample in the early part of this century when children frolicked in street clothes on the beach. This postcard was postmarked 1914. (Courtesy Elaine Pereira.)

Bathers in the breachway at Quonochontaug seem overdressed by our standards. The development of the area as a summer colony began about 1880. (Courtesy Elaine Pereira)

This group on the beach at Matunuck, probably from the 1920s, includes Joe O'Neil at front center. (Courtesy Mercedes McCabe.)

Narragansett Pier was always one of the more fashionable resorts along the South County coast. These bathers gathered on Sunday, August 10, 1902, according to a date on the back of the photograph. The beach may have been crowded that day because about 600 "excursionists," or day-trippers, had arrived in the Pier that day from Providence aboard the steamer *Warwick*. In the background of this photograph are the bowling alleys of Webster and Baur, run that season by William Cosgrove of Blackstone. Among the summer visitors who had recently arrived, according to *The Narragansett Times*, were John H. Holmes, owner of the *Boston Herald* and his son, John H. Holmes Jr., in town to watch the polo matches, and his employee J.J. McNamara, who was covering the tournament. A West Virginia senator and Bishop Thomas Conaty of Washington also had recently arrived to stay at the Imperial. (Courtesy Judith Babcock.)

This bathing attire is typical of the turn of the century. The Sears, Roebuck & Co. catalog of 1902 lists similar bathing costumes, made of alpaca (a type of wool) or brilliantine (a similar fabric with cotton warp and mohair or worsted filling). They featured detachable skirts, attached bloomers, and sailor collars. The costumes came in black or navy blue and were sold by Sears for $2.98 or $3.49, depending on the material. (Courtesy John W. Miller Jr.)

Imagine going to the beach in these getups, complete with dark stockings. In 1902, *The Narragansett Times* reprinted this sea-bathing advice from Good Housekeeping magazine: "Most of the benefits usually ascribed to sea bathing are due to the breathing of salt air. The ideal ocean bath comprises the plunge, the moment of benumbing cold, the immediately succeeding moment of irradiating warmth in which the strength of individual vitality asserts its supremacy over a destroying element, then the hard rub and quick run along the beach, by which means a possibly reluctant reaction is triumphantly realized." (Courtesy John W. Miller Jr.)

Bathing costumes for men were no more revealing than those for women. Sears, Roebuck & Co. in 1902 sold several styles similar to these, of cotton or worsted, with quarter-sleeve shirts and knee pants, again in black or navy. The price: 98¢ plain, $1.50 for stripes. (Courtesy John W. Miller Jr.)

In 1919 this group of beachgoers at Matunuck included the Kerwins, owners of Beacon Mills in New Bedford, MA, the McEvoys, the Harleys and the Durkins. Their dress indicates this may have been a spring or fall excursion. Note the rows of fishing shacks and the healthy expanse of dunes at Matunuck, which is now heavily eroded. (Courtesy Mercedes [Durkin] McCabe.)

A pyramid is on Narragansett Town Beach. John W. Miller Sr. is helping hold up the gang, shown here in the bottom row second from the left. Miller managed movie theaters in Wakefield and Narragansett, as well as the Narragansett Pier Casino. (Courtesy John W. Miller Jr.)

Umbrellas helped protect maidens and children from the sun along Matunuck Beach, where the Gould cottage can be seen in the distance. The cottage was located about where Roy Carpenter's trailers are today, on the south side of Matunuck Beach Road. (Courtesy Robert Beverly Hale Library.)

Play-ground, Pleasant View, R. I.

They called it Pleasant View; today we know it as Misquamicut. "Tents" were a common way to stay out of the sun while enjoying the ocean breezes. (Courtesy Elaine Pereira.)

This picture, dated 1898, shows Narragansett Pier in all its glory, before a devastating fire in 1900 destroyed the Rockingham Hotel and Casino and the automobile changed tourists' habits forever. (Courtesy Judith Babcock.)

The author's mother, Eleanor (Crandall) Thayer, poses for her sister Dorothy at Weekapaug in the summer of 1938. The dunes in the background would disappear a few months later when a savage hurricane ripped through South County. A student at what is now Rhode Island College, Miss Crandall, 18, met the hurricane's fury on a train headed out of Providence. She made it to Westerly, where she spent several days with her grandmother and had no way of letting her family know she was safe. (Courtesy Dorothy Crandall Bliss.)

Rachel E. Gilson poses with her daughter, Lee, on Matunuck Beach in 1946. Bathing attire reflected a more modern attitude during the post-war period. (Courtesy Lee Gilson Dursin.)

Canonchet Bathing Club, Narragansett, R. I.

18597

The Canonchet Bathing Club in Narragansett was a popular spot for bathers in the automobile era. (Courtesy Dot Smith.)

A teenage Wallace Burdick is shown on Charlestown Beach before the 1938 hurricane. Note the width of the beach and the number of summer cottages lining it. (Courtesy Barbara and Wallace Burdick.)

Three
ON THE WATER

Salt Pond, also known as Point Judith Pond, has played an important role in South County since before European settlement as a rich source of fish and shellfish. Today it is prized by boaters as well. (Courtesy Christine MacManus.)

WESTERLY, R. I.   Brightman's Pond.

We have Mrs Young for our teacher now and they like
2656 *her very much. How is George. I write you soon. D. J.*

Brightman's Pond in the Misquamicut section of Westerly has played a similar role in that town. As summer visitors began to flock to shoreline towns in Washington County, they were attracted to the pond shores as places for clambakes, games, and water sports, Lee notes in her research. This serene postcard is postmarked 1907. (Courtesy Christine MacManus.)

The salt ponds have been an important draw for summer visitors. Here Paul F. Casey, then ten years old, enjoys a row on Potter's Pond in 1941. Matunuck Point can be seen in the background. (Courtesy Marie Casey.)

Fishing shacks like these once lined Matunuck Beach, and the fishermen supplied the hotels and cottages that lined the shore. (Courtesy Elaine Pereira.)

Fishermen returning to Matunuck are greeted by shore bathers. (Courtesy Robert Beverly Hale Library.)

The advent of Galilee as a significant fishing port developed after the breakwater was built between 1892 and 1906 and a breachway to Point Judith Pond was dredged between 1902 and 1910. The name "Harbor of Refuge" is quite telling, for its initial purpose was to protect boaters from coastal hazards off Point Judith. (Courtesy Daryl Anderson.)

Point Judith Pond's role in fishing would change forever after 1900, when money was appropriated to dredge a permanent breachway between the pond and the ocean. According to research by Carl Gersuny and John J. Poggie Jr., some feared that the increased salinity would harm some species, and this prediction did come true. In her 1980 report on the salt ponds, researcher Virginia Lee of the University of Rhode Island's Coastal Resources Center noted that the breachway brought a severe decline in the pond's oyster fishery. (Courtesy Daryl Anderson.)

This view of Galilee shows the fishing shacks that once lined the port. (Courtesy Daryl Anderson.)

A woman in fancy dress at the turn of the century presents a sharp contrast to the lobster pots of Jerusalem. The village, located across the Harbor of Refuge from Galilee, retains its rustic appeal today. (Courtesy Daryl Anderson.)

This photograph, showing Jerusalem from the rocks at Galilee, shows how undeveloped that shore was compared to today. (Courtesy Daryl Anderson.)

The state and federal government funded the construction of state piers in Galilee and Jerusalem in the mid-1930s, and fish landings increased dramatically as a result. The Point Judith Fishermen's Cooperative, established in 1948, would play a key role in the port's development. The cooperative was designed to give fishermen control over the sale of their catch, eliminating the middleman, according to John Poggie and Carl Gersuny. (Courtesy Elaine Pereira.)

The Githens restaurant was located at the Port of Galilee. This picture appears to be from the 1930s. (Courtesy Daryl Anderson.)

Another view of the Port of Galilee shows hows its importance for tourism and recreation had begun to develop in the 1930s. The owners of these cars probably were patronizing Githens restaurant. (Courtesy Daryl Anderson)

Tom Doherty (left) congratulates Pierce Chappel (spelled thus on this photograph, although it may be Chappell) on his big catch. Recreational fishing has been a favorite sport in South County for generations. (Courtesy Daryl Anderson.)

Scallopers Henry T. Allen (left) and Henry Streeter come into Hanson's Boatyard in Wakefield on October 1, 1947, with the first catch of the season. Scallops began to thrive in Point Judith Pond after a permanent breachway was dredged to the ocean, increasing the pond's salinity, but recent years have seen few scallops in local salt ponds. (Courtesy Daryl Anderson.)

The coast of Narragansett Pier was filled with schooners, steamers, and coal barges in the years around the turn of the century, and visitors often arrived at the Pier on steamers from Providence. (Courtesy Christine MacManus.)

The Old Breakwater, Narragansett Pier, R. I.

This postcard shows the "old breakwater" at Narragansett Pier. (Courtesy Christine MacManus.)

Point Judith Pond, Wakefield, R. I.

Once an abundant source of oysters, perch, and alewives, Point Judith Pond played a strong economic role in South County. Today even its scallop fishery has declined severely, and its economic role is tied more to boating and tourism than fishing. (Courtesy Judith Babcock.)

Lew Stelljes and an unidentified woman enjoy a sail, probably on Point Judith Pond, while Ken Peckham and Bill Stedman (in stern) are out for a row. (Courtesy Daryl Anderson.)

Four

FARMS ALONG
THE SHORE

Farm hands working for potato farmer Hubert Kelley burn off plants to make way for the potato harvest in Charlestown. Kelley leased the fields from the Burdick family. Potato barns cropped up throughout South County in the late 1930s and 1940s as farmers made the transition from dairy farming. (Courtesy Charlestown Historical Society.)

A woman on the Burdick family farm shows off what would appear to be record-breaking squashes. Wallace Burdick, whose grandparents owned the farm, recalls that the Burdicks raised enough vegetables to feed their family all winter and supply all of Charlestown Beach's summer visitors as well. (Courtesy Charlestown Historical Society.)

Edward T. Burdick (1898–1935) shows off more gargantuan squashes at the family farm. (Courtesy Wallace and Barbara Burdick.)

Farmer Charles Henry Crandall (second from left) harvests seaweed on the Weekapaug shore with help from hired hand George Rathbun (standing on wagon). Crandall, the author's great-grandfather, used the seaweed to fertilize potatoes and corn on his District No. 6 farm in Westerly. The Crandalls were among several farmers who had seaweed-gathering rights written into their deeds. Crandall's grandson, Frank H. Crandall Jr., recalls his father telling him that competition among the farmers to gather the seaweed was fierce; after seaweed had been washed ashore by a storm, the farmers would cover their horses' hooves in burlap so other farmers would not hear them making their way to shore. The seaweed was spread on the fields in the fall and then plowed under in the spring after it had decayed. Descended from one of the town's original founders, Charles Henry Crandall was a prominent member of the Westerly community, active in Republican politics, and respected for his thriving trapping and farming enterprises. When he died in 1932, *The Westerly Sun* noted, "There was perhaps no man better known throughout southern Rhode Island and eastern Connecticut than the deceased." (Courtesy Dorothy Crandall Bliss.)

A Model A Ford came in handy at haying time on the Crandall farm in District No. 6, Westerly. Busy gathering hay were, from left to right, patriarch Frank Crandall Sr. and his sons, Frank Jr. and Charles (atop load). The Crandalls' Dunn's Corners Road farm included 130 acres, with 40 being meadow and garden crops. The farm also included cedar swamps, berry patches, and orchards. Frank Sr.'s daughter, Dorothy C. Bliss, recalled in her memoir *A New England Childhood* how especially prized were her father's melons: "In autumn when the melon crop was ripe, many relatives whom we had not seen all year stopped by knowing that our father would cut a watermelon or muskmelon (canteloupe)." (Courtesy Dorothy Crandall Bliss.)

This old gambrel-roofed farmhouse in Quonochontaug matches the description of the Sheffield House, built between 1685 and 1713 by Joseph Stanton. Although several farms were established in Quonochontaug in the 18th century, it would be another 100 years before the area became a summer resort. (Courtesy Elaine Pereira.)

Five

SAVING LIVES

OLD CASINO ARCH AND LIFE SAVING STATION, NARRAGANSETT PIER, R. I.

The Life Saving Station at Narragansett Pier, shown at left of the Towers, is now the Coast Guard House restaurant. The first crew began duty December 1, 1873, according to J.R. Cole's history of the county, at a station that cost $5,000 to build. The Life Saving Service performed a vital task in patrolling the coast for boaters in trouble. (Courtesy Dot Smith.)

The men of the Life Saving Service at Narragansett Pier are shown in this *c*. 1890s photograph. The crew was responsible for patrolling the shore on foot to watch for boaters in distress and used lifeboats like this to effect their rescues. (Courtesy Daniel G. Dunn.)

The Life Saving Service crew shown here inside their station at Narragansett Pier, which is now the Coast Guard House restaurant. The architectural details will be familiar to patrons of the popular restaurant. (Courtesy Daniel G. Dunn.)

A lighthouse has protected mariners at Point Judith since 1810; the present lighthouse, shown here, dates to 1857 and also was home to a Life Saving Station. In *The Reporter*, the quarterly journal of the Pettaquamscutt Historical Society, former crew member Clifford T. Gardner recalled his two years stationed at Point Judith with the Life Saving Service. "The day's routine at the station was always a busy one. There were two main duties: there was a man on watch in the tower at all times and the beach patrol was maintained all night long." The crew also helped the lightkeeper maintain the foghorn's air compressor. (Courtesy Elaine Pereira.)

THE WRECK, POINT JUDITH, NARRAGANSETT PIER, R. I.

The schooner *Harry A. Barry* came ashore February 19, 1887 near Point Judith. The following month, agent William C. Caswell advertised its contents and fittings to be sold at auction at the site near the Point Judith Lighthouse. The *Barry* apparently was carrying coal, as "coal scoops and all coal unsold" were among the items to be auctioned. This photograph shows what was apparently all that remained after the ship had been stripped and left to the ravages of time. (Courtesy Dot Smith.)

That same year, in November, the *Maggie J. Smith*, shown here, was grounded off Narragansett near the Dunmere estate after the captain mistook a light in a cottage window for the Beavertail lighthouse off Jamestown. The schooner also was carrying coal, 1,148 tons of it; *The Narragansett Times* reported that the vessel was only five years old and worth more than $30,000. Capt. Albert Church and his courageous crew at the Point Judith Life Saving Service was credited with rescuing the vessel's nine crew members that night, which was stormy with a southwest gale blowing and a high surf. William C. Caswell, the agent mentioned in the previous caption, was kept busy again stripping the vessel and selling its contents. *The Times* noted there was "not much prospect of ever getting her off" her grounding spot. (Courtesy Everett Hopkins.)

The wreck of the *Harry Knowlton* is seen here near Watch Hill, where it collided with the steamer *Larchmont* on Feb. 11, 1907. The *Larchmont* sank in 25 fathoms; the loss of life has been placed variously at 140 and 192. (Courtesy Elaine Pereira.)

The Coast Guard's Life Saving Service at Quonochontaug shows off the heavy oars of its patrol rowboat. The station, located on the west side of Quonochontaug Breachway, was staffed with a commander, seven men, and two boats. (Courtesy Charlestown Historical Society.)

The staff of the Life Saving Service at Quonochontaug practices firing lifelines. These lines were fired at boats in distress as a means of rescuing the crew. A Lyle cannon was used to fire the lines. (Courtesy Elaine Pereira.)

Beachcombers walk the shore in front of the Life Saving Station in Quonochontaug. (Courtesy Elaine Pereira.)

The staff of Quonochontaug's Life Saving Service poses for this photograph. The station, which dated to about 1890, patrolled from a point halfway west of the Charlestown Breachway to the breachway at Weekapaug. Clifford Pendleton, who served with the station, recalled in a history of Charlestown how the Hurricane of 1938 lifted the station's lifeboat and deposited it nearly undisturbed in the woods near Shady Harbor. (Courtesy Elaine Pereira.)

This photograph of the boathouse at Quonochontaug's Life Saving Service was taken between 1913 and 1915. Among the boathouse's equipment was a life car, a small contraption that distressed boaters were supposed to climb into before being pulled ashore. (Courtesy Elaine Pereira.)

The Watch Hill Lighthouse, the tall structure at right, was built about 1856 about 50 feet northwest of the original lighthouse. The first lighthouse was built of a wood and shingled design on land the federal government had purchased from George and Thankful Foster. The present structure, of Westerly granite, was built three stories high and equipped with a fourth order Fresnel lens. The radar station at left is no longer standing, the building behind it now houses a small museum and the light has been automated since 1986. (Courtesy Elaine Pereira.)

Here is another view of the Watch Hill Lighthouse. Since the early 19th century, watch towers at this site have helped save mariners caught in storms off rocky Watch Hill Point. (Courtesy Elaine Pereira.)

Lifeguards Robert Frederick "Don" Smith, Howard Goodchild, and George Gilson guarded the shores of Matunuck from their lifeguard chair in 1941. The three would be cited for heroism in their rescue of two Newport socialites whose plane crashed off the beach in July of that year. All three young men would later die in World War II. (Courtesy Lee Gilson Dursin.)

George Gilson and a young boy examine the wreckage of a plane that crashed off Matunuck Beach in the summer of 1941. Gilson and fellow lifeguards Don Smith and Howard Goodchild pulled Eleanor Young and Nicholas S. Embiricos from the plane, but both later died of their injuries. (Courtesy Lee Gilson Dursin.)

The anchor motif on the Coast Guard's Life Saving Station at Narragansett Pier can be seen in this postcard. The building eventually was converted to a restaurant that today pays homage to the Coast Guard through its name. This photograph was taken before an addition was built onto the structure (Courtesy Dot Smith.)

Catherine Durkin and her son James examine a shipwreck that was a familiar fixture off Matunuck Beach. This photograph was taken in the summer of 1921. A number of schooners had run aground in that vicinity before that time, including the *Oakwoods* and the *Blue Jay*. (Courtesy Mercedes McCabe.)

THE BEACH, LOOKING EAST, MATUNUCK, R. I.

The same shipwreck can be seen on Matunuck Beach in this postcard. When such wrecks came ashore, residents often carried the coal off in buckets. (Courtesy Robert Beverly Hale Library.)

Six

AMUSEMENTS

Charlestown Beach cottagers wait for the mail at this beachside post office. Sending and receiving letters took on great importance when vacationers spent months at a time by the sea. (Courtesy Christine MacManus.)

The Casino at Atlantic Beach, Pleasant View, R. I.

This casino at Atlantic Beach in Pleasant View, what is now known as Misquamicut, was a center of activity. In her memoir *A New England Childhood*, Dorothy Crandall Bliss included diary entries from the Hurricane of 1938. "Such buildings as the Atlantic Casino are nothing more than a few stubs," she wrote as early reports came to them from the shore. Photographs showed the casino was badly damaged, but not swept away. (Courtesy Elaine Pereira.)

Maine's I Scream, established in 1884 in Wakefield, brings its ice cream to the beach at Narragansett Pier in this undated photograph. The store's delivery wagons were made by C.H Armstrong and Sons, a carriage works in Wakefield. (Courtesy Daniel G. Dunn.)

Bathing Pavilion, Narragansett, R. I.

This bathing pavilion at Narragansett Town Beach was one of many that have graced the Pier's beautiful waterfront. (Courtesy Dot Smith.)

Casino Dance Hall, Narragansett Pier, R. I.

This casino and dance hall was built after Narragansett Pier's first casino was leveled in a 1900 fire. The site of everything from fancy dress balls to bridge parties, it was a social focal point in the age of the automobile. In 1915, *The Narragansett Times* reported on the casino's opening for the season by detailing its orchestras, chefs, and managers. Fireworks and dancing would inaugurate the season, the *Times* reported, and the culinary department would be headed by Julian Sere of Sherry's in New York. Among the social highlights that year would be the Black and White Ball to benefit the New York Herald Ice Fund. (Courtesy Dot Smith.)

The Golf Club House at Watch Hill was a very popular spot. Golf was an integral part of resort life, and resorts measured their success by the quality of their golf courses. In 1898, *The Narragansett Weekly* listed three golf courses in Westerly—the Misquamicut, in Watch Hill; the Farmleigh Links; and a new club being organized at Noyes Beach called the Weekapaug. That summer the Watch Hill club had hired an 18-year-old professional from Scotland, Harrie Reddie, who soon broke a course record. The season was sometimes inaugurated with a tea, which may have been the occasion of this photograph. (Courtesy Elaine Pereira.)

Polo was another center of social activity in Narragansett Pier. This postcard, postmarked 1910, shows the game being played at the Point Judith Country Club. Among the teams that played in Narragansett were the Philadelphia Country Club, Camden Grasshoppers, the Great Necks, Bryn Mawr, and Cooperstown. (Courtesy Christine MacManus.)

This water carnival on Brightman's (Winnapaug) Pond in Misquamicut drew a crowd of spectators. (Courtesy Elaine Pereira.)

Members of the Gilson family get ready for a game of croquet at "The Hedges," Atlantic Avenue, Matunuck in August 1942. They are, from left to right, Irving T. Gilson, Lee Gilson, and their mother, Rachel E. Gilson. (Courtesy Lee Gilson Dursin.)

This bowling alley at Quonochontaug floated across the pond in the Hurricane of 1938 and its pins and alleys were found days later in the woods, pretty much intact. (Courtesy Elaine Pereira.)

Known as the Ocean Star Cottage, this farmhouse of George N. Browning on Card's Pond Road in South Kingstown began accepting visitors in 1891. Its tally-ho coach was a popular feature, taking guests on excursions to such places as Narragansett Pier and Point Judith. Browning's wife continued to operate the inn after his death, until 1919, and then Leonard and Alyce Tyler purchased it in 1921 and converted its barn into a theater that opened in 1933. Today we know it as the ever-popular Theatre-by-the-Sea. (Courtesy Laura Harris.)

This early picture shows an outbuilding at what would become Theatre-by-the-Sea. The Tylers first ran the farm as a summer camp before converting it to a theater. Over the years, stars drawn to the picturesque theater would include Fay Wray, Mae West, Buddy Ebsen, Will Geer, and Talullah Bankhead. (Courtesy Laura Harris.)

This postcard, postmarked 1941, shows the theater after repairs in the wake of the Hurricane of 1938, when its roof blew across the road. The 1941 season, which included *George Washington Slept Here* and *Pursuit of Happiness*, was the theater's last before World War II forced the owners to lower the curtains. Live theater did not return to Matunuck until 1946. (Courtesy Marie Casey.)

Quocompaug Lodge, Charlestown, R. I.

Quocompaug Lodge in Charlestown was apparently a rustic retreat in the hills of Charlestown. Quocompaug is the Native-American word used to refer to Schoolhouse Pond and the spring that feeds it. (Courtesy Elaine Pereira.)

Seven

GRAND HOTELS

The Towers was the grandest of the grand—an archway that stretched across Ocean Road to greet summer visitors to Narragansett Pier. It has survived two fires and changing times, one of the last reminders of the Pier's tourism heyday. (Courtesy Linda Stedman.)

S.W. Mathewson operated this hotel, the Mathewson, the largest in Narragansett Pier. In a directory published by the Hotel Men's Association, the hotel's healthful aspects were stressed. "Sanitary arrangements pronounced perfect by Sanitary Inspectors and Medical Experts," proclaimed its advertisement, which also noted that the hotel was supplied with "absolutely pure Spring Water, flowing from the noted 'Mathewson Spring.'" (Courtesy Daniel G. Dunn.)

The Green Inn opened in 1888 at the corner of Ocean and South Pier roads in Narragansett, a four-story hotel with 50 rooms open year-round. The inn burned in 1980 and has since been replaced by private residences modeled after it in architecture. (Courtesy Dot Smith.)

Carlton Hotel, Narragansett Pier, R. I.

The Kinney Lodge, which eventually became the Carleton Hotel, was an imposing presence on Ocean Road. Cigarette maker Francis Kinney built it as his private residence in 1896. It was later converted to a hotel and by 1940 it was being run by Angelo F. Joy. (Courtesy Dot Smith.)

The Breakers and Atlantic Hotels, Narragansett, R. I.

The Breakers and the Atlantic House were twin hotels on Ocean Road in Narragansett Pier; the Atlantic House still stands. Built in 1866-67, it boasted 87 rooms. In The *Narragansett Times*' "A Sketch of Narragansett Pier," the Atlantic House was said to have every modern amenity. "The dining hall is one of the coziest and coolest at the Pier," *The Times* wrote. "In the large double parlors which front upon the lawn is a large fireplace, so that a cheerful open fire can temper the chill of the morning air for those guests who wish to remain during September. Electric bells are in every room and the house is supplied with hot or cold sea water baths." (Courtesy Dot Smith.)

Beachwood Hotel, Narragansett, R. I.

The Metatoxet House dated to 1856 and was renamed the Beachwood after Elizabeth Wood purchased it. In a hotel directory for 1891, proprietor John H. Caswell noted that a new music room had been added and the hotel's water came from the Wakefield Water Works. Wood operated the Beachwood until 1936, according to historian Oliver Stedman; by 1940, its proprietor was Samuel A. Tourjee. In June of that year he advertised, "Rooms $1.50 per person up; ala carte dining room; cocktail lounge; special attention paid to luncheons and bridges."

The Massasoit Hotel, Narragansett, R. I.

The Massasoit Hotel at Narragansett Pier accommodated 130 guests and featured wrought-iron fire escapes, an important feature in the age of wooden hotels. (The hotel burned in 1971.) In 1891, with John Babcock as manager, the hotel boasted "sleeping rooms [that] are large and arranged for comfort, with wide, airy halls." (Courtesy Dot Smith.)

Built in 1854 and later moved to this site, Revere House was the first establishment built for the purpose of taking in boarders at the Pier, according to J.R. Cole's history of Washington and Kent counties. It was considered a huge gamble in the days when a stagecoach was the only way to get to the Pier. Later the Narragansett Pier Railroad would forge a quicker connection to the train station in Kingston. (Courtesy Dot Smith.)

Ocean Road in Narragansett Pier was a row of hotel after hotel, all facing the Atlantic breezes. (Courtesy Dot Smith.)

The Hotel De La Plage was originally the Continental Hotel in Narragansett Pier on Ocean Road; it was renamed after it was moved to Beach Street. The Continental opened in 1871 and boasted accommodations for nearly 200 guests in four stories. In an 1888 sketch of Narragansett Pier, its proximity to the ocean was described thus: "In fact, the waves beat against the rocky shores at its very gates, only the avenue lying in between." (Courtesy Dot Smith.)

The Longfellow House in Matunuck was among many popular boarding houses and cottages that sprang up along the beach near the turn of the century. When she visited in 1893, Mariana Tallman of *The Providence Journal* noted that Matunuck was popular with Providence residents "more so, perhaps, than any other surf beach on our coast," although at the time "there is nothing, absolutely nothing, there but one hotel, a half-dozen bathing houses, and the ocean." (Courtesy Elaine Pereira.)

The Park House in Matunuck was run by Albert Clark; his daughter, Marjorie, later married historian Oliver Stedman, according to James E. Perry Sr.'s memoir, *I Remember*. (Courtesy Elaine Pereira.)

The Matunuck Beach Hotel was built about 1880 by Wanton Carpenter of Perryville and added on to in 1884 and 1895. In his *I Remember*, James E. Perry Sr. recalls that Arthur Carpenter ran the hotel and his brother Wanton operated a large boarding house of his own just south of the Perryville Baptist Church. Perry characterized the Matunuck Beach Hotel as "a rather large facility" whose chief feature was the large verandas on the lower and upper floors. Here guests "could get a splendid view of the sea, with the passing ships, and [could] enjoy the cool summer breeze that swept across the 'Weeden Farm' to the south west." The hotel was destroyed in the Hurricane of 1938. (Courtesy Everett Hopkins.)

Atlantic House, Matunuck, R. I.

The Atlantic House in Matunuck, now the Narragansett Salt Water Fishing Club, was among several popular boardinghouses and hotels in that settlement. (Courtesy Robert Beverly Hale Library.)

The Marilla was a popular summer boardinghouse at the corner of Prospect and Ocean Avenues in Matunuck that rented housekeeping units; it was named for Marilla Barney. Here visitors could cook their own meals (among each apartment's furnishings in 1903 were a "spider, skillet, [and] five-quart tin kettle") or take their meals at nearby hotels. (Courtesy Robert Beverly Hale Library.)

George I. Champlin and his wife, Etta Jane (Tucker) Champlin, founded the popular Dewey Cottage on Matunuck Beach Road in Matunuck. (Courtesy Joan W. Nippo.)

George I. Champlin and his wife, Etta, opened the Dewey Cottage to Matunuck boarders in 1898. Today it has been restored as the Admiral Dewey Inn. (Courtesy Robert Beverly Hale Library.)

The Buena Vista was operated in Matunuck by C.B. Champlin. During the 1902 season, *The Narragansett Times* wrote glowingly of the fun to be had at this establishment: "A jolly crowd made the walls of Buena Vista ring during all of the past week . . . The height of the fun was reached on Thursday night, when midst the cheers of an admiring audience a ping pong tournament was held . . . Plans are under way for a series of such 'evenings' which are expected to enhance the ever-growing reputation of Buena Vista as one of the most popular cottages at Matunuck." (Courtesy Elaine Pereira.)

The Ocean View Hotel, listed as at Charlestown Beach, was included among the casualties in Quonochontaug during the Hurricane of 1938. The distinction between the two resorts was sometimes blurred. (Courtesy Elaine Pereira.)

The Sea Breeze Inn in Quonochontaug was operated by Mimmi Nurmi when this postcard was printed and boasted "all sports, fine home cooking, reasonable rates." (Courtesy Elaine Pereira.)

The Mount Pleasant section of Quonochontaug in Charlestown is shown here in this postcard. The development of a summer colony at Quonochontaug—often spelled "Quonocontaug" at this time—began in the 1880s. (Courtesy Elaine Pereira.)

The Misquamicut Inn was actually in Watch Hill. In his 1878 history of Westerly, "Westerly and its Witnesses," Reverend Frederic Denison was effusive in his praises of Watch Hill: "For ocean scenery, for bathing, for fishing, for quiet, for health, Watch Hill has no superior on our coast." (Courtesy Elaine Pereira.)

Among the grandest hotels at Watch Hill was the area's first, Watch Hill House. Jonathan Nash, who had been the first lightkeeper at Watch Hill Lighthouse, built the hotel about 1833. By 1889, when J.R. Cole was writing his history of the county, the hotel consisted of 178 rooms, and the property included 165 feet of beach frontage. "The house is well equipped in every particular, and is most handsomely located on the hill, affording a good view of the surrounding scenery," Cole wrote. (Courtesy Elaine Pereira.)

Eight
SUMMER COTTAGES

COPYRIGHTED 1906 BY ED. N. BURDICK.

View of Bay. Watch Hill, R. I.

The development of Watch Hill as a summer colony dates to the early 19th century. Closer to New York than South County's other resorts, it was accessible by steamer and trolley. Of the steamers, the *Block Island* was the largest, traveling between Norwich and Block Island, and the *Ella* the second largest, traveling between Norwich and Watch Hill. (Courtesy Elaine Pereira.)

The Wigwam, Pleasant View, R. I.

Pleasant View (what we today know as Misquamicut) also became a popular spot on which to build summer cottages. The beautiful stonework of the Wigwam was a landmark until the Hurricane of 1938 damaged it. In a 1922 brochure listing cottages for rent, agent Frank W. Coy listed a "Wigwam" at Watch Hill as having five "sleeping rooms," a butler's pantry, and servants' bath, among other rooms. This cottage—it's unknown if it was the same Wigwam pictured here—rented for $1,800 a season, a princely sum in the early 1920s. (Courtesy Elaine Pereira.)

THE PIONEER & WIGWAM COTTAGES, PLEASANT VIEW, R. I.

The Pioneer cottage is shown in the foreground, the Wigwam beyond it. In its coverage of the 1938 hurricane, *The Westerly Sun* described the Wigwam as a hotel and noted that an unnamed cottage next to it, owned by George Phillips of Providence, also was damaged. (Courtesy Elaine Pereira.)

More summer cottages are shown along the shores of Pleasant View, which boasted a casino and trolley connection from Westerly. (Courtesy Elaine Pereira.)

Cottagers at what appears to be Charlestown Beach stroll along a boardwalk. Note the hammock on the porch and the gentlemen's formal dress, *de rigueur* no matter how casual the occasion. (Courtesy Christine MacManus.)

The Midway cottages at the east end of the Quonochontaug summer colony; the strip would later be devastated by the Hurricane of 1938. (Courtesy Elaine Pereira.)

The Ashaway was a colony of cottages at Quonochontaug, perhaps named for the Hopkinton village of the same name. (Courtesy Elaine Pereira.)

By 1880, 14 cottages had been built at the west end of Quonochontaug, known as the Heights and pictured here. (Courtesy Elaine Pereira.)

Church's Charlestown Beach was a rustic retreat in 1912, the postmark of this postcard. The Church family owned a portion of the beach. For many years the Burdick family owned a large tract of land clear to the ocean, and even as summer people began flocking to the shore, once a year the Burdicks would close a gate on what is now Charlestown Beach Road to maintain its status as private property. (Courtesy Christine MacManus.)

Creek Bridge on Charlestown Beach Road forded Green Hill Pond when the area was virtually undeveloped. (Courtesy Charlotte Brophy.)

COTTAGES ON MOON STONE BEACH, MATUNUCK, R. I.

This postcard is labeled "Moon Stone Beach," but it looks more like the area to the east, which we know as Browning's Beach. The postmark is 1911. (Courtesy Elaine Pereira.)

The Simeon Whitford family reposes on the porch of Moonstone Cottage, located just west of the end of Moonstone Beach Road in South Kingstown. Seated is Simeon Whitford. His oldest daughter, Hannah, shown standing beside him, was the grandmother of Everett Hopkins, who recalls his mother saying that his grandfather, John Hopkins, named the cottage—and thus the beach— "Moonstone," because at night the full moon glittering on the pebbles made them look like the jewel of the same name. John Hopkins, like his grandson, was a teacher and at one point taught at a Narragansett Indian school. He eventually sold the cottage and bought property at Moonstone Beach Road and Matunuck Schoolhouse Road he dubbed "Little Moonstone Camp." An icehouse was located to the north of this cottage on Card's Pond and the family had seaweed rights to the shore. Seven cottages at Moonstone Beach, including this one, were destroyed during the Hurricane of 1938; today the land, save one lot to the east, is part of the Trustom Pond National Wildlife Refuge. (Courtesy Everett Hopkins.)

This Noyes Beach was a section of Matunuck; another Noyes Beach was located in Westerly. (Courtesy Elaine Pereira.)

In this cottage in Matunuck, artist Frank Convers Mathewson (1862–1941) returned each summer to paint the South County scenery he so loved. He discovered Matunuck while visiting the summer home of one of his pupils in 1910 and returned to buy a house on Old Post Road. An honorary president of the South County Art Association, he frequently traveled to Europe to paint, and one of his watercolors hung in the Paris Salon. (Courtesy Elaine Pereira.)

The True family enjoys an outing at Charlestown Beach *c.* 1895–1900. The first cottages in South County were built along the barrier beach at Charlestown Pond and then wiped away in a 1912 storm, according to Virginia Lee's *An Elusive Compromise.* (Courtesy Christine MacManus.)

The coming of the automobile changed summer visitors' habits forever. No longer was a visit to South County available only to those who could afford to lease, or build, a summer cottage. In this photograph motorists pitch tents at Cronin's Bathing Beach off Ocean Road in Point Judith. (Courtesy Elaine Pereira.)

Roy Carpenter's Beach, Matunuck, R. I.

After World War II, improved road systems brought more visitors to the South Shore. Tiny cottages like these at Roy Carpenter's Beach in Matunuck were now in the financial reach of the burgeoning middle class. This postcard was postmarked 1953. (Courtesy Elaine Pereira.)

The Allview Cottage, also known as Barney's Pagoda, was one of the more unusual structures in Matunuck. (Courtesy Robert Beverly Hale Library.)

Nine

CLAM SHACKS AND LUNCHEONETTES

Charlestown Grist Mill, Cross Mills, R. I., at junction of Route 2 and U. S. Route 1

Long before tourists discovered the South Shore, South County corn meal was prized as the base of many a tasty jonnycake and gristmills were an important economic force from the dawn of European settlement. Cross' Mills boasted two—this mill, opened by Benjamin Gavitt in 1930, and one across the road at the intersection of Route 2 and Old Post Road. The former was the site of a gristmill as early as 1709. By 1877, when William F. Tucker was writing his sketch of Charlestown, Alfred Collins and Benjamin B. Greene were its owners. The gristmill in this building was dismantled in 1952 and the building was operated as a store by Mr. and Mrs. Frederick Main. This postcard, postmarked 1948, notes, "This is the little country store where we bought corn meal." (Courtesy Elaine Pereira.)

Browning's Lunch and "Nation Wide Store"

Browning's Lunch and Nationwide Store was opened in this farmhouse on Old Post Road in Charlestown, next to what is now the Mini-Super, sometime before 1919. Grace (Hoxsie) Browning began selling canned goods out of the 1777 farmhouse and her husband, Robert Browning, supplied the store's vegetables, eggs, and other farm goods. A series of additions were built to accommodate the growing enterprise and eventually the Brownings' son, Perry Browning, took over the business. In a 1962 interview with a *Providence Journal* reporter, Perry Browning said, "A lot of the folks who come in here I've known since I was a boy. Most of the adults who shop around for penny candy I knew as kids when they came around doing the same thing." (Courtesy Elaine Pereira.)

This is what Browning's Store looked like after it was closed in 1969. The building has since been dismantled. (Courtesy Charlestown Historical Society.)

A row of businesses developed along Bay Street in Watch Hill as its popularity as a summer resort grew. This area is known as Mastuxet Terrace. (Courtesy Elaine Pereira.)

Among the businesses on Bay Street in Watch Hill was Sisson's Restaurant, operated by Mrs. Olaf Berentsen. Upstairs the restaurant offered "rooms with running hot and cold water." (Courtesy Elaine Pereira.)

Otis E. Brown ran a grocery out of this building at far right in Quonochontaug. Grocery stores, livery stables, bowling alleys, and ice cream parlors were among the many businesses that cropped up along the shore to serve summer visitors. (Courtesy Elaine Pereira.)

The Worcester House Garage most probably served the Worcester House, one of a string of hotels along Quonochontaug that were destroyed in the 1938 hurricane. (Courtesy Elaine Pereira.)

Mother Brindley's establishment in Quonochontaug, variously referred to as an ice-cream parlor and store, was so popular its spot was known as "Mother Brindley's Corner." In her history of Charlestown, Frances Wharton Mandeville referred to the emporium as "a famous gathering place in summer before the 1938 hurricane." (Courtesy Elaine Pereira.)

Catherine Durkin is shown at Holland's Store with her sons, James and Bill, in May 1928. This building on Matunuck Beach Road was one of a complex of structures, including three other cottages, which were owned by the Crandall family in Matunuck. When the property was broken up in 1920, Dr. James Durkin bought one cottage and another dentist named Dr. Cooney bought adjacent "twin" cottages. The store went to the Harley family. (Courtesy Mercedes McCabe.)

The Point Judith Coffee House (later the Lighthouse Inn restaurant) and Ideal Picnic Grounds were a popular spot in Narragansett. This postcard was probably made in the late 1920s or 1930s; it has a 1939 postmark. Today the inn is boarded up but the scenic overlook, next to the Point Judith Lighthouse, is known as Rose Nulman Park and is as popular as ever. (Courtesy Elaine Pereira.)

The popular Aunt Carrie's restaurant in Point Judith, still a favorite among clam-cake lovers, also had tourist cabins when this photograph was taken. The restaurant dates to 1920. (Courtesy Elaine Pereira.)

Ten

THE GREAT STORMS

Houses along Charlestown Beach are shown devastated by the Hurricane of 1938. On September 21, 1938, when a tropical storm bearing winds of up to 120 mph barreled into Rhode Island, it carried with it profound social and economic change. Summer colonies from Watch Hill Point to Narragansett Pier were wiped off the map. (Courtesy Charlestown Historical Society.)

Employees of a drugstore in Narragansett Pier managed to escape the rising waters of the Hurricane of 1938 after this photograph was taken. This rare view of the storm at its height shows the Narragansett Post Office and theater to the right. "In Narragansett proper the water poured in with such suddenness that it caught businessmen and passersby totally unprepared," reported *The Narragansett Times*. "Motorists abandoned cars. Storekeepers fled. Shoppers departed in flight." (Courtesy J.A. Coggeshall.)

The Charlestown Beach Hotel was among the cottages and hotels that were blown to smithereens by the Hurricane of 1938. In a book published shortly after the storm, The Federal Writers' Project of the Works Progress Administration reported that Charlestown Beach "has been wiped clean of human habitation." At some points sand was piled 8 to 12 feet deep, and for days the grim search for bodies was carried out. (Courtesy Charlestown Historical Society.)

Houses line East Beach in Charlestown before the great storm of 1938. In a booklet published a month after the hurricane, *The Westerly Sun* reported that Quonochontaug had lost 214 cottages in the gale and Charlestown Beach, 185. Farther to the north, along Charlestown Pond and in Charlestown by the Sea, 104 homes were destroyed, *The Sun* reported. (Courtesy Charlestown Historical Society.)

Labeled "West Beach, Charlestown," this photograph probably shows the Quonochontaug section before the 1938 hurricane took most of the cottages away. The death toll from the storm was estimated at 45 in the Charlestown-Quonochontaug area. (Courtesy Charlestown Historical Society.)

Built in 1888, the Eldridge House was a popular hotel on Quonochontaug Beach owned by Thurman Eldridge and his wife, Elizabeth (Maude), who also owned the resort's bowling alley and clam shack as well as a summer cottage. Sensing the storm was to be a bad one, Eldridge came down to his summer property on September 21, 1938, to retrieve a strongbox of money from the hotel. He, his wife, and their son John narrowly escaped death. At one point a house came blowing down the road toward them as they tried to make their escape on foot. They were saved by an older son, Charles, who rescued them in a rowboat and took them to the nearby Kenyon farmhouse. (Courtesy Elaine Pereira.)

This is probably the Kenyon farmhouse where the Eldridge family retreated in 1938 to escape the hurricane. The storm killed an estimated 45 people in the Quonochontaug and Charlestown Beach areas, destroying the Eldridge's hotel as well as the Ocean View Hotel, Worcester House, and Breakers Hotel. (Courtesy Elaine Pereira.)

Fort Mansfield Road in Watch Hill was a thin stretch of commodious summerhouses in 1938. Named for the Spanish-American War–era fort that had been built at its tip, of which only concrete walls remained, the road would be erased in an estimated 15 minutes by waves 30 feet high. One cottage was floated to a nearby island, its residents clinging on for dear life. *The Westerly Sun*, calling the road "one of the most exclusive streets of this resort" in a booklet published after the hurricane, reported that 15 residents died and 44 houses were destroyed in this Napatree Point area. In all, the hurricane claimed 53 homes in Watch Hill. (Courtesy Elaine Pereira.)

This postcard shows another view of the Fort Mansfield area that was destroyed in 1938. The photograph was taken from the Plimpton Hotel built by S.A. Plimpton & Co. in 1865. (Courtesy Elaine Pereira.)

This is what the garage at the Crandall Farm on Dunn's Corners Road looked like in the wake of the Hurricane of 1938. In her memoir *A New England Childhood*, Dorothy Crandall Bliss recalled how her father and brother braved the hurricane winds to retrieve a car and tractor from the garage as the building threatened to collapse. "We saw the building sway perilously and we screamed at the men to forget the tractor," she wrote. "At about the same time, they noticed that the building was going to crash. They grabbed the bar and together pulled the tractor out to what they hoped was a safe place." (Courtesy Dorothy Crandall Bliss.)

Martial law was declared after the hurricane to keep order and prevent looting. Here officers at East Beach in Quonochontaug restrict access to the stricken beaches. (Courtesy Elaine Pereira.)

This is what homeowners would find once they were able to return—those lucky enough to have lived through the Hurricane of 1938. (Courtesy Elaine Pereira.)

Weekapaug Inn — Weekapaug, Rhode Island.

The Weekapaug Inn presents a grand appearance in this pre-1938 photograph. After the storm it would look like a child's dollhouse that had been ripped open by Godzilla. A new breachway the storm cut through to Quonochontaug made the inn a virtual island, and the five people who had taken shelter in the inn were rescued by a 27-year-old lifeguard, Henry Morris, who swam across the channel five times to carry them to safety. The west side of the inn was destroyed, its boathouse and garages were washed away and the hotel suffered severe exterior damage. In Weekapaug, one person died and 23 homes were leveled. (Courtesy Elaine Pereira.)

The Dunes Club at Narragansett Pier bore the brunt of the damage because of its shore location. Reported *The Narragansett Times*: "Hugh Donnelly was in a cabana at the Dunes Club with a companion, when a huge wave swept away the section in which they were seeking refuge. He was reported missing, as his companion appeared." The area suffered an estimated $2 million in damage in the Hurricane of 1938 and 18 people died. (Courtesy J.A. Coggeshall.)

This is what the Dunes Club swimming pool looked like the day after the Hurricane of 1938 roared through. *The Narragansett Times* reported that the dunes between the club and the Narrow River had been flattened by the storm. (Courtesy J.A. Coggeshall.)

Sherry's Bathhouse at Narragansett Pier also was destroyed in the 1938 storm. A number of other beach structures in the Pier, including the Beach Corporation bathhouse and Palmer's bathhouse, were leveled, some carried as much as 50 yards away. (Courtesy J.A. Coggeshall.)

Ocean Road in Narragansett was strewn with rocks from the sea wall in the wake of the 1938 hurricane. This view was taken the day after the storm. (Courtesy J.A. Coggeshall.)

Boats at Point Judith (Salt) Pond were piled up like toys by the 1938 gale, and the docks at the head of the pond were destroyed. (Courtesy J.A. Coggeshall)

The fishermen of Galilee were hard hit by the 1938 storm. Reported *The Narragansett Times*, a week after the hurricane: "Fishermen in many instances lost everything they possessed in connection with their occupation . . . But real tragedy struck at Sand Hill Cove and the Breachway. The damage is unbelievable. The entire squatter's section of houses has been carried away. There remains nothing but sand and rock with no indication of a settlement of any kind." (Courtesy Elaine Pereira.)

Charlie Carpenter's Mobil station in Narragansett Pier is shown here, probably in the late 1930s, surrounded by cars parked for the beach. (Courtesy Daryl Anderson.)

The same gas station after hurricane winds ripped it open. The back of the photograph is dated September 18, 1944, so this damage may be from the storm of that year. (Courtesy Daryl Anderson.)

Fishermen would refloat their boats, property owners would rebuild cottages, villages would re-emerge after 1938, only to have more damage inflicted by Hurricane Carol in 1954. This photograph shows a Matunuck cottage known as "Blue Dormers" after it was gutted by a tidal surge. (Courtesy Lee Gilson Dursin.)

Hanson's Boatyard in Wakefield, located at the head of Point Judith (Salt) Pond, was a sea of wreckage after Carol's devastating visit on Aug. 31, 1954. The storm carried wind gusts of up to 115 mph. (Courtesy Lee Gilson Dursin.)

Eleven

SCENES ALONG THE SHORE

This early view of Narragansett Pier—believed to date to the 1860s—shows the beach at a time when its identity as a shore resort was just beginning. Travelers still had to take a stagecoach to reach the beach, and only a few hotels and boardinghouses existed to accommodate them. (Courtesy John W. Miller Jr.)

Another view of the Narragansett Pier beach before pavilions began to line its shores. This undated photograph is probably from the mid- to late 19th century. (Courtesy John W. Miller Jr.)

OLD MAN'S FACE, NARRAGANSETT PIER, R. I.

The Old Man's Face in Narragansett was among a number of rocks that became landmarks to visitors of the area. Others included Sunset Rock and Indian Rock. (Courtesy Dot Smith.)

This street scene in Narragansett Pier, probably from the 1920s, shows stores selling such items as bathing suits and luggage. (Courtesy Dot Smith.)

What a contrast downtown Narragansett was in this postcard, when it was a bustling collection of brick buildings housing restaurants, shops, and hotels. The victim, or benefactor, of urban renewal—depending on your view—Narragansett's downtown was razed in the late 1970s and early 1980s. Today, only the post office, shown at right, still stands. (Courtesy Dot Smith.)

The Old Mill in Narragansett was located at the Rockledge estate. (Courtesy Dot Smith.)

St. Philomena's Church, a Catholic chapel, was located on Rockland Street in Narragansett. Increasing summer populations often prompted the establishments of summer chapels. (Courtesy Dot Smith.)

This aerial view of Narragansett Pier shows the area just east of the Towers. The landscape is almost unrecognizable because of urban renewal, but one landmark that still remains is the Narragansett Post Office at the top right. (Courtesy Daryl Anderson.)

This section of Matunuck Beach Road was called Beach Street when this postcard was made, probably pre-1920. (Courtesy Elaine Pereira.)

Even Matunuck, though it was sometimes derided for its slower pace, had a boardwalk. (Courtesy Robert Beverly Hale Library.)

Several accounts place this post office at the junction of what is now Route 1 and Matunuck Beach Road. In a 1923 article in *The Narragansett Times*, Thomas A. Gardiner recalled that William R. Weeden helped establish the area's first post office, which soon was moved to a variety store owned by the Goodchild brothers. A few years later it was moved to Holberton's store, presumably this building, built in 1871. The establishment of a post office was a clear indicator of Matunuck's up-and-coming status as a shore destination. (Courtesy Everett Hopkins.)

This old mill, whose remains can be found at Colonial Mill Farm on Moonstone Beach Road, is believed to have made stockings for soldiers in the Civil War. The mill is referred to in one account as shoddy mill, which means it used reclaimed wool. According to Everett Hopkins, another building on the property was used to process the wool. The building shown here burned in the 1920s. (Courtesy Everett Hopkins.)

The Samuel Perry House on Matunuck Schoolhouse Road is one of the oldest homes in South Kingstown. Dated to the late 17th century, the house was in the Perry family until 1809 and was restored in 1957. (Courtesy Everett Hopkins.)

The students of the District No. 12 schoolhouse are shown in this 1894 photograph. The schoolhouse was located just north of the Carpenter Gristmill on Moonstone Beach Road. Its teacher at this time was Alvin Card (center rear), who also was Matunuck's first rural free delivery carrier. The following students, from Perryville, are, from left to right: (front row) Frank Card, Leroy Carpenter, and Howard Browning; (second row) Mabel Browning, Rubbin Clarke, Myrtle Gould, Arthur Jackson, and Jessie Gould; (third row) Mauld Grinnell, Julia Whitford, Hattie Grinnell, Reba Grinnell, Inish Grinnell, ? Grinnell, ? Hazard, ? Hazard, and Charlie Wright; (back row) Louis Perry, Millie Cashman, Mr. Card, Mabel Whitford, and Ella Clarke. Looking out the window is Earl Carpenter. (Courtesy Everett Hopkins.)

Benjamin and Wanton R. Carpenter's store stood at the corner of Old Post Road and Moonstone Beach Road in Perryville. This photograph is believed to date to 1862. The Carpenters have played an important role in the Matunuck and Perryville area as farmers, hotel operators, and business owners. (Courtesy Everett Hopkins.)

Arnolda was established as a residential compound in Charlestown by Thomas L. Arnold and Frank W. Arnold of Brooklyn, NY, who bought the Champlin, Foster, and Greene farms around 1905. The Arnold brothers, who had deep Rhode Island roots, became enchanted with Charlestown's rustic character while visiting their sister, whose husband owned King Tom Farm. By 1976, when the town's history was published for the bicentennial, Arnolda included 32 houses. The homes were built on large lots, many fronting on Charlestown Pond, with narrow, winding lanes affording the homeowners plenty of privacy. Frank Arnold also developed Arnolda East, near Cross' Mills. Both are now year-round communities. (Courtesy Elaine Pereira.)

The Village Post Office, Charlestown, R. I.

This post office was one of many established over the years in and around Cross' Mills. Before Route 1 bypassed the village and town business moved to a new town hall on Route 2, Cross' Mills was the town's commercial center. (Courtesy Elaine Pereira.)

The Ocean House was among the earliest shore resorts built in Charlestown. Dated variously to 1846 or 1848, it was built on the shores of Charlestown Pond by James and George Ward and included a public hall, Ward's Hall, that was divided up when Peleg Sisson bought the property in 1871. Among its notorious summer visitors was Rufus Brown Bullock, a Reconstruction governor of Georgia who started spending his summers at the Ocean House shortly after the Civil War ended. Bullock, who was indicted on corruption charges but later acquitted, went on to become president of the Atlanta Cotton Mills. His wife, Marie Salisbury, was a native of Pawtucket, which probably accounts for their summering here. He is credited with launching a sailboat race on Charlestown Pond in 1876 that was named after him. The Ocean House, now home to the Ocean House Marina, was known as Cold Brook Farm at the turn of the century after a spring in the area. (Courtesy Charlestown Historical Society.)

Cross Hall, at the intersection of Old Post Road and Route 2, served an important public function when it was built in 1855. According to William F. Tucker's sketch of Charlestown, town councils met in a public hall in its upper story until 1876. The basement housed a store and post office. The building remains a landmark in Cross' Mills. (Courtesy Charlestown Historical Society.)

The District No. 1 schoolhouse, now an art gallery, was built in 1843 and underwent substantial renovations in 1874. After the school closed in 1923 it was used as the Charlestown Community Club. William F. Tucker, in his historical sketch of Charlestown, had this to say about the school: "From 1845 to 1860, perhaps no school in the town excelled this one in literary attainments; and in reference to teachers, without doubt this school has produced nearly as many as all the other schools combined." (Courtesy Elaine Pereira.)

This photograph purportedly shows the airship *Hindenburg* flying over Charlestown Pond on its way to a rendezvous with fate in Lakehurst, NJ, on May 6, 1937. *The Westerly Sun* reported the day after the dirigible's explosion that it had passed over Westerly at about 1:30 in the afternoon, about five hours before it reached New Jersey. "The ship was riding above the fog and was obscured from the view of those on the ground," *The Sun* reported on May 7. "The sound of the motor resembled several airplanes. The Hindenburg passed over Providence at 12:25." The fiery crash killed 32 people. (Courtesy Daniel G. Dunn.)

Bathing Beach. Watch Hill, R. I.

The bathing beach at Watch Hill is shown in this photograph, probably pre-1938. In 1898, *The Narragansett Weekly* listed the resort's attractions thus: "It is on the mainland, and easy of access from New York or Boston. It has water on three sides, hence it is almost always cool. The ground is high, and the place is free from diseases of all kinds." (Courtesy Elaine Pereira.)

The Square. Pleasant View, R. I.

When Misquamicut, or Pleasant View, was connected to a trolley line out of Westerly, a resident wrote on the back of this postcard: "The Westerly road is just behind the trolley car and leads off to the right where you sketched the hay stacks. This green patch on the left is my 'back yard.' So you see we are right in the centre of things. Regular Exchange Place in fact." (Courtesy Elaine Pereira)

Avondale, R. I.

This is Avondale, which until 1893 was known as Lotteryville because it had been settled through a lottery. Federal regulations forced the name change when a post office came to town. In its guide to Rhode Island, the Federal Writers' Project noted the area was once "an important boat landing." (Courtesy Elaine Pereira.)

Pawcatuck River. Westerly, R. I.

The train tracks hug the shore of the Pawcatuck River in Westerly, which forms the Rhode Island-Connecticut border. (Courtesy Elaine Pereira.)

View on Ocean Avenue, showing Mastuxet and Ninigret Lodges, Watch Hill, R. I.

This view of Ocean Avenue in Watch Hill shows the Mastuxet and Ninigret lodges. By 1878, when Reverend Frederic Denison was writing his history of Westerly, Watch Hill's large hotels included the Watch Hill House, the Atlantic House, the Plimpton House, the Ocean House, the Narragansett House, the Larkin House, and the Bay View House. (Courtesy Elaine Pereira.)

The Watch Hill Post Office is shown at right in this photograph. "Every sojourner becomes acquainted with the Post Office soon after his arrival," noted *The Narragansett Weekly* in 1898. That year W.N. York was postmaster. The resort also had several telegraph offices in its hotels. (Courtesy Elaine Pereira.)

Several features are worth noting in this postcard of Bay Street in Watch Hill. They include the trolley line running down the roadbed; the businesses on the south side of the street, which is mostly open to Little Narragansett Bay now; and the carousel at the far end of the street, which still entertains the younger set. The trolley in 1898 was run by the Pawcatuck Valley Street Railway, which connected with trains at the Westerly station and made trips out of Watch Hill every half-hour. (Courtesy Elaine Pereira.)

This view of Watch Hill is looking toward Aquidneck Avenue. Note the windmill and water tower in the background. (Courtesy Elaine Pereira.)

This house, dating to 1665, is the original homestead of Elder John Crandall, a founder of Westerly. Crandall built a one-room cabin on this land, purchased from Chief Sosoa of the Misquamicut tribe, and it remained in the Crandall family until recently when the house—subsequently added on to—and a substantial parcel were granted to the Narragansett Indian tribe. (Courtesy Dorothy Crandall Bliss.)

The cottages of Pleasant View can be seen way in the background; note the absence of trees. Pleasant View is today known by its original American Indian name of Misquamicut, which means salmon. (Courtesy Elaine Pereira.)

Sprague Bridge in Narragansett crossed Narrow River; it can still be seen south of the present bridge on Boston Neck Road. This postcard, postmarked 1936, notes: "Caught a flounder this morning, but it jumped out of the bag." (Courtesy Dot Smith.)

119

Githens restaurant sold lobster dinners and clam cakes right on the shore in Galilee. (Courtesy Daryl Anderson.)

Mary, Paul, and Charles Casey pose in front of their Aunt Angela and Uncle Bob Farrell's house on Matunuck Beach Road in 1941. Summers were carefree for youngsters. (Courtesy Marie Casey.)

Sand Hill Cove at one time was a collection of "squatters' houses," or small camps used in the summer. It was wiped clean by the Hurricane of 1938. (Courtesy Daryl Anderson.)

These fishing shacks at Galilee are in sharp contrast to the bustling commercial port of today. (Courtesy Daryl Anderson.)

This view, dated 1869, shows how treeless Narragansett Pier was—with a view all the way to Tower Hill House at what is now the campus of Msgr. Matthew F. Clarke School. Central Street is in the foreground. (Courtesy Daryl Anderson.)

Edward T. Burdick employs a little horsepower on the Burdick farm in Charlestown, located near Charlestown Beach. (Courtesy Wallace and Barbara Burdick.)

View of Narragansett's Famed Towers
Narragansett, R. I.

The Towers in Narragansett is the most recognizable feature of the town's heyday to remain. Designed by McKim, Mead and White, the Towers burned in the 1900 fire that also razed the adjacent casino and the Rockingham Hotel. Another fire and hurricane damage have beset the building over the years, but the massive structure has undergone substantial renovation. The leatest plans call for the restoration of the cupola, which was destroyed in a 1965 blaze. (Courtesy Dot Smith.)

This aerial photograph shows Hazard castle at Sea Side Farm, now Our Lady of Peace, located on Ocean Road in Narragansett Pier. The castle and tower were built by Joseph Peace Hazard. (Courtesy Daryl Anderson.)

Two people enjoy a sail, probably on Point Judith Pond. Carefree days on the pond have started many a love affair with South County. (Courtesy Daryl Anderson.)

A last look at Point Judith, or Salt, Pond. The water continues to draw thousands of visitors to the South County resort towns of Narragansett, South Kingstown, Charlestown, and Westerly. (Courtesy Daryl Anderson.)

BIBLIOGRAPHY

Allen, Everett S. *A Wind to Shake the World: The Story of the 1938 Hurricane.* Boston: Little, Brown and Company, 1976.

Amory, Cleveland. *The Last Resorts.* New York: Harper and Brothers, 1948.

Barrett, Shirley L. "The Hales of Matunuck: Distinguished Summer Residents." *The Reporter*, Quarterly Journal of the Pettaquamscutt Historical Society, Summer 1986.

Bliss, Dorothy Crandall. *A New England Childhood.* Salem, MA: Higginson Book Company, 1997.

"Carol Was Here." Wakefield: *The Narragansett Times*, 1954.

The Charlestown Bicentennial Book Committee. *Reflections of Charlestown, 1876–1976, A Memorial to The Bicentennial Celebration of the United States of America.* Westerly: The Utter Company, 1976.

Cole, J.R. *History of Washington and Kent Counties, Rhode Island.* New York: W.W. Preston and Co., 1889.

Denison, Reverend Frederic. *Westerly and its Witnesses, 1626–1876.* Providence: J.A.and R.A. Reid, 1878.

Federal Writers' Project of the Works Progress Administration for the State of Rhode Island. "Rhode Island, A Guide to the Smallest State." *American Guide Series.* Boston: Houghton Mifflin Company, 1937.

Federal Writers' Project of Works Progress Administration for the New England States. *New England Hurricane: A Factual, Pictorial Record.* Boston: Hale, Cushman and Flint, 1938.

Gardner, Clifford T., as told to Shirley L. Barrett. "The Life Saving Service at Point Judith." *The Reporter*, the Quarterly Journal of the Pettaquamscutt Historical Society, Autumn 1987.

Gardiner, Thomas A. "The Early Postal Services of South Kingstown." Originally printed in *The Narragansett Times.* September 1923. (Excerpted and edited by Shirley L. Barrett for *The Reporter*, the Quarterly Journal of the Pettaquamscutt Historical Society, Winter 1988–89.)

Garraty, John A. and Mark C. Carnes, eds. *American National Biography, Vol. 3.* New York: Oxford University Press, 1999.

Gersuny, Carl and John J. Poggie Jr. *Harbor Improvement and Fishing at Point Judith.* Unattributed article in vertical file of Peace Dale Library.

———. *Fishermen of Galilee, the Human Ecology of a New England Coastal Community.* Narragansett: University of Rhode Island Marine Bulletin Series Number 17, 1974.

Greene, Lewis R. and William A. Cawley. *The Hurricane, Sept. 21, 1938, Westerly, Rhode Island and Vicinity, Historical and Pictorial.* Westerly: The Utter Company, Printers, 1938.

Jackson, Henry. *An Account of the Churches in Rhode Island,* presented at the adjourned session of the 28th annual meeting of the Rhode Island Baptist Convention, Providence, November 8, 1853. Providence: George H. Whitney, 1854.

Latimer, Sallie. *Narragansett By-The-Sea.* Dover, N.H.: Arcadia Publishing, 1997.

Lee, Virginia. *An Elusive Compromise: Rhode Island Coastal Ponds and their People.* Narragansett: Coastal Resources Center, University of Rhode Island, Marine Technical Report 73, 1980.

Mandeville, Frances Wharton. *The Historical Story of Charlestown, Rhode Island, 1669–1976.* Charlestown Historical Society, 1979.

Narragansett Pier, R.I. Narragansett: The Hotel Men's Association, 1891.

The Narragansett Times. 18 November 1887; March 1887; July 4, 1904; August 8, 1902; August 15, 1912; July 2, 1915; July 23, 1915; July 30, 1915; September 30, 1938; May 24, 1940; June 28, 1940.

The Narragansett Weekly. June 30, 1898; July 7, 1898; July 14, 1898; July 21, 1898; August 4, 1898.

Perkins, P.J. *Shipwrecks, Sinkings and Strandings from Narragansett and South Kingstown, 1880 through 1940.* Unpublished manuscript, 1993.

Perry, James E. Sr. *I Remember, Recollections of Growing Up in South Kingstown, 1899–1972.* Privately printed.

The Providence Journal. March 27, 1938; July 1, 1941; July 2, 1941; December 25, 1941; and May 29, 1944.

Rhode Island Historical Preservation Commission, State of Rhode Island and Providence Plantations. *Preliminary Survey Report: Town of Charlestown.* Providence: Rhode Island Historical Preservation Commission, 1981.

———. *Preliminary Survey Report: Town of South Kingstown.* Providence: Rhode Island Historical Preservation Commission, 1984.

Sears, Roebuck catalog, 1902 edition. Reprinted, with an introduction by Cleveland Amory. New York: Bounty Books, 1969.

Seavor, Jim. "That's Entertainment in Matunuck." *The Providence Journal,* undated clipping.

"A Sketch of Narragansett Pier, Its Past, Present and Future." *The Narragansett Times,* 1888.

Stedman, Oliver. *A Stroll Through Memory Lane.* West Kingston: The Kingston Press, 1978.

"The Storm of the Century: 60th Anniversary Edition, the Hurricane of 1938." Supplement to the *South County Independent,* September 17, 1998.

Tallman, Mariana. "Pleasant Places in Rhode Island." *The Providence Journal,* 1893.

Tucker, William Franklin. *Historical Sketch of the Town of Charlestown, in Rhode Island, from 1636 to 1876.* Westerly: G.B. and J.H. Utter, Steam Printers, 1877.

The Westerly Sun. February 25, 1932; May 7, 1938; and September 25,1938.